HOT TOPICS

TERRORISM AND SECURITY

Nick Hunter

Heinemann
LIBRARY

Chicago, Illinois

www.heinemannraintree.com
Visit our website to find out
more information about
Heinemann-Raintree books.

To order:
☎ Phone 888-454-2279
🖳 Visit www.heinemannraintree.com
to browse our catalog and order online.

© 2012 Heinemann Library
an imprint of Capstone Global Library, LLC
Chicago, Illinois

Visit our website at www.heinemannraintree.com

Edited by Adam Miller, Andrew Farrow, and
Jennifer Locke
Designed by Clare Webber and Steve Mead
Original illustrations © Capstone Global Library
Ltd.
Picture research by Ruth Blair
Production by Eirian Griffiths
Originated by Capstone Global Library Ltd.
Printed and bound in China by Leo Paper Group
Ltd.

16 15 14 13 12
10 9 8 7 6 5 4 3 2 1

**Library of Congress Cataloging-in-Publication
Data**
Hunter, Nick.
Terrorism and security / Nick Hunter.—1st ed.
    p. cm.—(Hot topics)
 Includes bibliographical references
and index.
  ISBN 978-1-4329-4873-3 (hc)
 1. Terrorism. 2. Terrorism—Prevention.
 3. Civil defense. I. Title. II. Series.
  HV6431.H87 2012
  363.325—dc22   2010044764

Acknowledgments
The author and publishers are grateful to the
following for permission to reproduce copyright
material: Alamy pp. **11** (© Imagestate Media
Partners Limited – Impact Photos), **21** (© S.
Forster), **26** (© scenicireland.com/Christopher
Hill Photographic), **31** (© Stacy Walsh
Rosenstock), **36** (© Trinity Mirror/Mirrorpix), **38**
(© Jeffrey Blackler); Corbis pp. **5** (© HO/Reuters),
6 (© Les Stone/Sygma), **8** (© Bettmann), **13**
(© Patrick Robert/Sygma), **15** (© Reuters), **17**
(© Scotland Yard/Handout/Reuters), **22** (©
MOHAMMED SABER/epa), **27** (© Ron Sachs/
CNP/Sygma), **32** (© CHIP EAST/Reuters), **35**
(© Peter Macdiarmind/POOL/epa), **42** (© David
Furst/Pool/epa), **43** (© Ed Darack/Science
Faction), **47** (© Sheng Hong/Xinhua Press),
49 top (© Reuters), **49** bottom (© DESMOND
BOYLAN/Reuters); Getty Images pp. **19** (JIJI
PRESS-JSDF/AFP), **24** (Chip Somodevilla), **29**
(CHRISTOPHE SIMON/AFP), **45** (John Moore);
Shutterstock p. **41** (© Iryna Rasko).

Cover photograph of a surveillance camera
reproduced with the permission of Science Photo
Library (Cordelia Molloy).

We would like to thank Kristen Kowalkowski for
her invaluable help in the preparation of this
book.

Every effort has been made to contact copyright
holders of any material reproduced in this book.
Any omissions will be rectified in subsequent
printings if notice is given to the publisher.

Disclaimer
All the Internet addresses (URLs) given in this
book were valid at the time of going to press.
However, due to the dynamic nature of the
Internet, some addresses may have changed,
or sites may have changed or ceased to exist
since publication. While the author and publisher
regret any inconvenience this may cause readers,
no responsibility for any such changes can be
accepted by either the author or the publisher.

CONTENTS

Some words are printed in bold, **like this**. You can find out what they mean by looking in the glossary.

PANIC OVER DETROIT

Flight 253 from Amsterdam was starting its final descent into Detroit, Michigan. Most passengers had returned to their seats, and fastened their seatbelts. Suddenly there was a bang like a "balloon being popped." People could see smoke and flames coming from one of the seats and passengers and crew wrestling with a man who seemed to be on fire. At this stage few of them knew how close they had come to disaster.

The commotion was caused by Umar Farouk Abdulmutallab. As the plane prepared to land, he had tried to detonate explosives that were hidden in his pants. If he had been successful, the explosion may have been enough to bring down the airplane, along with its 290 passengers and crew. Fortunately, the device did not explode, and the quick reactions of the people closest to the bomber prevented a disaster.

Background of the bomber

Once the plane had landed safely, and the badly burned Abdulmutallab had been arrested, details began to emerge about his background. Abdulmutallab was from a wealthy Nigerian family. He was known to be a follower of a radical form of Islam and had links to members of the al-Qaeda terrorist network in Yemen. His father had been worried about his son's behavior and had contacted the U.S. Embassy to say that he might be involved in terrorist activities.

Abdulmutallab's attempted bombing was just the latest incident in a campaign of attacks that had been launched against United States and other Western targets by followers of radical Islam and al-Qaeda, led by Osama Bin Laden. The use of explosives strapped to the bomber's body was a new tactic, but targeting an airplane with the aim of killing as many people as possible was nothing new.

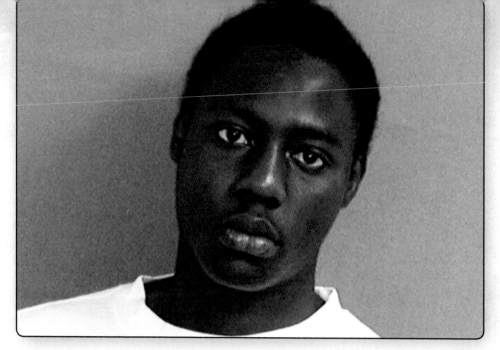
Abdulmutallab was restrained by the passengers and crew of Flight 253 until the plane landed safely and he could be arrested.

Looking at terrorism

This kind of deliberate attack on **civilians** is known as terrorism. Many people have lost their lives in recent terrorist attacks, and governments around the world have put huge resources into tackling the terrorist threat. This book will look at the methods used by terrorists and ask why people resort to terrorism and how they can be stopped. It will also consider many of the issues and debates surrounding terrorism and ask if terrorism can ever be justified.

"It was terrifying. We all thought we weren't going to land; we weren't going to make it. We were in the back of the plane and all of a sudden heard some screams and some flight attendants ran up and down the aisles. We saw the fear in their eyes and they grabbed the fire extinguishers."

Richelle Keepman, a passenger on Flight 253, *The Observer*, December 27, 2009

WHAT IS TERRORISM?

Terrorism is a very powerful word. It brings up images of innocent people killed and maimed in bomb blasts and shootings. There are images on the news every night of the latest terrorist attack. It could be in your own country or somewhere more distant. We see images of burning buildings or shocked survivors. Reporters and politicians use words like **atrocity**, massacre, and outrage. We are left in no doubt that the terrorist attack is a terrible crime.

■ The bombing of the Federal Building in Oklahoma City, Oklahoma, in 1995 was at that time the biggest terrorist attack on U.S. soil. Some 168 people died in the attack, which was carried out by Timothy McVeigh, a white U.S. citizen with extreme **racist** views.

But do we know what terrorism is? There are a number of wars and conflicts going on around the world. Is terrorism always different from war, or can it be happening at the same time? Terrorists are usually described as a "network," "unit," or "cell," which suggests that they are well organized and trained. Is this always the case?

There is no single definition of terrorism, although governments and international organizations like the **United Nations** have their own definitions. Most definitions of terrorism cover three different aspects:

- *What is it?* Terrorist acts are generally considered to be violent acts carried out against a **civilian** population. Many people would say that terrorist acts can also be carried out against military personnel—for example, the bombing of a barracks where soldiers are sleeping and not actively fighting a war.

- *Who does it?* Most definitions used by governments say that terrorism is carried out by unofficial groups rather than governments. Many people also believe that governments can be responsible for terrorism if they commit violent actions designed to terrorize people. This kind of terrorism is called state terrorism. This book will focus on terrorism carried out by individuals and small groups.

- *Why do they do it?* Most people agree that terrorist acts are carried out to achieve some kind of political or religious aim, or to have an influence on governments and the people who vote for them.

"War on Terror"

In 2001, U.S. President George W. Bush declared a "war on terror" following the attacks of September 11, 2001, that killed more than 3,000 people in New York, Washington, D.C., and Pennsylvania. This war has mainly been waged against countries and groups that support or carry out terrorist attacks in the name of radical Islam. These groups are important, but they are far from being the only groups responsible for terrorism, as we can see if we take a look at how terrorism has developed in the twentieth and twenty-first centuries.

Terrorism is certainly not new. There have been terrorist attacks throughout history. Many of the earliest terrorists had religious motives. A group called the "Assassins" carried out attacks in the Middle East between the eleventh and thirteenth centuries. They believed in the necessity of purifying Islam. They would become part of the inner circle of politicians and religious leaders and then murder them. The killers would then wait to be arrested and executed for their actions. Much like **suicide bombers** in the modern world, they thought that death would earn them rewards in the afterlife.

We use the word *assassin* today to mean someone who murders people for political reasons. There were also groups from other religions who believed that they were doing the work of their god by murdering those who did not believe what they believed.

TERRORISTS OR FREEDOM FIGHTERS?

Whether someone is a "terrorist" or not can depend on your point of view. No one ever describes themselves as a terrorist. Those who the media calls terrorists believe that they are fighting for a just cause, even though the methods they use to fight appear unjustified and brutal to those who oppose them or who are neutral observers. Most terrorist groups have some supporters whom see them as fighting for freedom.

■ The Arab-Israeli conflict has often led to terrorist attacks around the world. Eleven Israeli athletes were **kidnapped** by Palestinian terrorists at the Munich Olympic Games in 1972. Nine of the athletes and five of the terrorists were killed in an attempt to rescue the **hostages**.

CASE STUDY

The Arab–Israeli conflict

Anyone wanting to understand terrorism in the modern world needs to know about the reasons for the conflict between Arabs and Israelis in the Middle East. After World War II, when at least six million Jews had been murdered in the Holocaust, the United Nations voted to partition (divide) Palestine to create a Jewish homeland in the Middle East. The Palestinians opposed this, and a bitter war followed between the new state of Israel and its Arab neighbors. Many Palestinians were forced to leave their homes in 1948 and became **refugees**.

There is still conflict between Arabs and Israelis. Palestinians fight to reclaim land that they see as rightfully theirs. Israel fights to protect itself against Palestinians and Arab nations that the Israelis believe would destroy Israel if they could. Terrorist acts have been committed on both sides of the conflict. Palestinians say that they have no choice but to use **guerrilla** warfare against the Israelis. Others say they are terrorists.

Politics and nationalism

In the nineteenth century, new political systems and ideas started to spread. Groups wanting political change began to develop. Many peoples around the world were part of the empires built up by European countries such as Great Britain, France, Germany, and Austria. These people wanted to govern themselves. This **nationalism** caused many to turn to terrorism.

Religion, political causes, and nationalism have continued to be the main reasons for terrorism in the modern world. Often, there are aspects of all three in terrorists' motivations.

CASE STUDY

Country terrorism

We also need to remember that countries can sometimes be responsible for terrorism. This is when governments break their own laws to terrorize people who disagree with them. Sometimes governments try to justify this by saying that they are doing it to protect their citizens from terrorists and others who would harm them. We will look in more detail at how governments react to terrorism later in this book.

The birth of today's terrorism

In the twenty-first century, if people talk about terrorism, they generally mean terrorism carried out by radical **Islamist** groups like al-Qaeda. Although there are many other terrorist groups, they often only threaten one country or region. Some Islamist groups have declared **jihad**, or holy war, on the West and have launched attacks in North America, Europe, and elsewhere. Where did these groups come from?

We have already seen that the Arab-Israeli conflict has led to terrorist groups developing in the Middle East. Attacks by Palestinian groups were often launched in Europe. This was partly because a worldwide television audience created publicity for the Palestinian cause. It was also because many in the Middle East believe that European countries and the United States favor Israel in the conflict.

There were two events in 1979 that played an important part in the development of Islamist terrorism. The first was the Iranian Revolution, which replaced Iran's ruling shah (king), who was friendly to the West, with a fundamentalist Islamic government. This government supported Islamic fighters across the Middle East. In November 1979, radical students stormed the U.S. Embassy in Iran, taking 66 people hostage. This showed the new government's hostility to Western involvement in the region.

The Kurds in Iraq

Iraq, led by its former president, Saddam Hussein, was guilty of state terrorism on many occasions. Any opposition was brutally suppressed by Saddam. In the most infamous event, he accused Iraq's Kurdish people, who lived in the north, of siding with Iran in a war between the two countries. So he used chemical weapons against the Kurds. More than 5,000 civilians died when chemical bombs were dropped on the town of Halabja in March 1988.

Jihad in Afghanistan

The other event was the invasion of Afghanistan by the Soviet Union. The tribal leaders of Afghanistan fought a fierce war to drive the invaders out of their country. Muslim leaders across the Middle East declared a jihad and urged young Muslims to go and fight in Afghanistan. The Afghan fighters were supported by Western and Arab countries. The invaders were driven out in 1989, and many of these fighters returned to their countries determined to fight on behalf of Muslims everywhere. One of these fighters was a wealthy young man from Saudi Arabia named Osama Bin Laden.

■ Some countries have provided support for terrorists when it serves their political interests. Libya has often been accused of supporting terrorists, most notably after the bombing of a U.S. airplane over Lockerbie, Scotland, in 1988, in which 270 people died. Libya agreed to stop its support for terrorism in 2003.

Al-Qaeda

Since the 1980s, al-Qaeda has grown to become the most powerful terrorist group in the world, with links to different groups stretching around the globe.

In 1989, after the Soviets had been expelled from Afghanistan, most of the fighters who had come from across the Muslim world drifted back to their homes. Osama Bin Laden started to form the group that became known as al-Qaeda. It was planned that those who had fought in Afghanistan would form an "international army" to defend Muslims.

Bin Laden returned to Saudi Arabia. When Saddam Hussein's Iraq invaded Kuwait in 1990, Bin Laden offered to use his al-Qaeda fighters to defend Saudi Arabia. But the Saudi rulers chose to seek help from the United States and its allies. This infuriated Bin Laden, who left his home country for Sudan and then Afghanistan, where al-Qaeda took shape.

OSAMA BIN LADEN (1957–2011)

Osama Bin Laden was born in Riyadh, Saudi Arabia. His father was a wealthy businessman who died when Osama was 11 years old. Teachers say that he was "shy, retiring, gracious, and courteous" as a boy. He was a devout Muslim, and while at the university he was exposed to radical Islam. This had a big influence on his life, and, when the Soviet Union invaded Afghanistan, he went to defend the country. After a time in Saudi Arabia and Sudan, Bin Laden returned to Afghanistan in 1996 and released statements urging Muslims to liberate the holy sites from Western influence. Following the attacks of September 11, 2001, Bin Laden went into hiding and would occasionally release messages to his supporters. On May 2, 2011, Bin Laden was killed in Pakistan by U.S. special forces. It is still unclear what effect his death will have on al-Qaeda.

■ The first that many people in the West heard of Bin Laden and al-Qaeda was the bombing of the U.S. Embassies in Dar Es Salaam, Tanzania, and Nairobi, Kenya, in 1998.

"The Base"

Al-Qaeda means "the base" in Arabic. It was not a tight-knit group controlled day-to-day by Bin Laden. As the name suggests, al-Qaeda provides a base for many different groups. Until 2001, it was able to provide training, weapons, and money for different terrorist groups from its camps on the mountainous border between Afghanistan and Pakistan.

Since the attacks on September 11, 2001, al-Qaeda has changed. Al-Qaeda's fighters have been at war with the United States and its **allies** in Afghanistan, so they have not been able to provide the training and money for terrorist groups that they did before 9/11. The "base" has also been greatly disrupted by Bin Laden's death, but the danger remains from groups that see themselves as following the methods and aims of al-Qaeda.

What are the aims of al-Qaeda?

- Re-establish one ruler or *caliph* for the whole Muslim world
- Remove Western influence from the House of Islam, particularly the holy sites of Makkah and Medina
- Destroy Israel and the Jews
- Replace corrupt Muslim regimes that have helped the West to extend its influence over the Muslim world

TOOLS AND TACTICS

Terrorists use lots of different weapons to achieve their goals. Although it sometimes seems like terrorists just want to kill and injure innocent people, their aims are usually more complex than that and this determines the weapons they use. Individual attacks are designed to have a number of specific effects:

- Cause terror in civilian populations. If people fear terrorist attacks, they may put pressure on their governments to agree to terrorist demands.
- Cause widespread damage and disruption that will be costly and difficult to repair and might change a government's policy.
- Create maximum publicity for their cause. Mass media can broadcast TV pictures around the world by satellite or online. This means that attacks can get instant publicity.
- Recruit more people for their cause. Although many people will be repelled by terrorist attacks, those who agree with their views may see them as heroic freedom fighters.

"Skyjacking"

In 1970, Palestinian terrorists **hijacked**, or "skyjacked," three passenger airplanes over Europe. The planes were flown to an airfield in Jordan, where the passengers were released but the airplanes were blown up. Live TV pictures of the explosions were beamed around the world and created a lot of publicity for the Palestinian cause. Of course, many people thought these actions were unacceptable and turned against the Palestinians, but the terrorists gambled that if they could show themselves to be capable of such attacks, governments and people overseas were more likely to listen to what they had to say.

Attacks against airplanes and other means of transportation create terror around the world because so many people travel. More than 60 airplanes were hijacked in 1971, but skyjacking gradually became less popular with terrorists as governments introduced new security measures and became less likely to negotiate with the hijackers.

Planes as weapons

Since 2001, plane hijacking has taken a sickening twist. There had been bombs on planes before (see page 11), but on 9/11, passenger airplanes were used as missiles. They were flown into the World Trade Center in New York City and the Pentagon in Washington, D.C. Another plane intended for Washington crashed in Pennsylvania after passengers fought with their attackers.

The huge loss of life on 9/11 showed that terrorists were prepared to mount attacks that would cause the most casualties. Since then, there have been calls for armed security guards on flights, and there have been very few hijackings. Terrorists know it is highly likely that any hijacked plane will be shot down to prevent casualties on the ground. Many terrorists are not prepared to die in their attacks. Security at airports and on planes is also much tougher than it was before 2001.

Hostages

Hostage taking is also a tactic that has been used frequently. Hostages are often held for months or years, and this can focus attention on an issue for a long time. In recent years, governments have put a news blackout in place when hostages are taken, asking the media not to give the captors publicity. This denies the terrorists one of their main goals, which is to get media coverage. Hostages are often used to bargain for the release of terrorist prisoners.

A grim development in recent years has been the use of the Internet by hostage takers. There have been examples of executions being filmed and shown online. Again, the terrorists believe that the publicity and fear that this causes is more valuable to them than the fact that even some of those who support their campaign would be appalled.

■ After the hijacking in 1970, Palestinian militants were forced to leave Jordan, which was unhappy about its land being used for such attacks.

Bombing

Bombs are probably the most common weapon used by terrorists. From a terrorists' point of view, a large bomb that can cause a huge amount of destruction is relatively easy and inexpensive to produce.

Economic destruction

One of the main goals of terrorist groups is to cause economic damage to their enemies. Terrorists reason that large-scale destruction, or even just the threat of it, will cost their enemies more than they are prepared to spend, so they will give in to the terrorists' demands.

During the 1980s and 1990s, the **IRA**, whose aim was to unite Northern Ireland with the rest of Ireland, placed large bombs in towns and cities across the United Kingdom. These were normally detonated at times when the areas were less busy. Lots of civilian deaths would have hurt their cause, but the IRA hoped the cost of reconstructing parts of cities like London and Manchester would weaken the resistance of the British people and government. Although the campaign was designed to cause destruction and disruption to buildings and businesses, many people also lost their lives in these attacks.

Massive car and truck bombs have been familiar during the recent conflicts in Iraq and Afghanistan. U.S., U.K., and allied forces in those countries have not been the only targets; civilians have also been targeted with these bombs. Partly this is because of conflict between different groups within the population. These bombings are designed to make life unbearable so that people will turn against the Western forces that are **occupying** their country.

Suicide bombers

It has become more common for terrorists to sacrifice their own lives in order to take the lives of others. The terrorists who attacked the United States on 9/11 did not expect to survive. Suicide bombers might be driving a car packed with explosives or, as in the case of Flight 253 (see page 4), carrying a bomb onto a plane.

Many suicide bombers are simply people, sometimes women and children, with explosives strapped to them, which are then detonated in a public place, causing death and injury to those around them. Islamist terrorist groups call this **martyrdom**, and they and radical ordained religious leaders who support them say that martyrdom will lead to paradise. Most Muslims believe that this is a warped reading of the teachings of Islam.

CASE STUDY

Suicide bomber: Shehzad Tanweer

Shehzad Tanweer detonated a bomb on an underground train in London on July 7, 2005, killing himself and seven other people. Tanweer had lived in and around Leeds, England, all his life. Friends described him as a "good Muslim" and a "nice lad." No one suspected that he might become a suicide bomber.

In late 2004, Tanweer traveled to Pakistan for three months, where he visited family and attended a madrassa (Islamic school). He was accompanied by Mohammad Sidique Khan, who is thought to have been the leader of the four suicide bombers who struck London's transportion system, killing 52 people and injuring hundreds. Tanweer and Khan were both known to the security forces but were not thought to be an urgent threat.

■ This photo (taken with a security camera) shows three of the suicide bombers who attacked the London transportation system on July 7, 2005.

Weapons of Mass Destruction

As we have seen in this chapter, the methods that terrorists use change over time. For those whose job is to fight terrorism and protect the public, the greatest worry is that terrorists will gain access to new and more dangerous weapons.

Weapons of Mass Destruction (WMDs) include chemical, biological, and nuclear weapons. A number of countries hold these weapons, and there is a real fear that the weapons could get into the hands of terrorists. Up to now, there have only been very small incidents of chemical and biological agents being used in terrorist acts.

Although there is always a possibility that terrorists might use WMDs if they got hold of them, we also know that, for the most part, terrorists have clear goals. Terrorists look to cause panic and to get publicity. An attack using WMDs would alienate many of their supporters, and the global community would almost certainly reply to such an attack with much greater force than was used after the events of 9/11.

One of the terrorists' greatest weapons is fear itself. Although many people have been killed, the fear of terrorism has had a much bigger impact on how we live than any single terrorist act. The next question to ask is, what are terrorists trying to achieve with the fear and publicity created by their actions?

Terrorism in context

There is no doubt that governments and the public see terrorism as one of the most serious issues we face. However, compared to other causes of death worldwide, terrorism is way down on the list. In 2001, more than 3,000 people died in international terrorist attacks. Since then, the annual death toll from international terrorism, excluding civilians killed in the Iraq and Afghanistan conflicts, has been less than 1,000. In comparison, more than 1 million people die every year in car accidents.

ROGUE COUNTRIES

Intelligence agencies and governments are continually watching those countries that either have weapons of mass destruction and might provide them to terrorists or are trying to develop them, such as North Korea and Iran. There are also more individuals than ever before who have the knowledge to produce Weapons of Mass Destruction if they have the materials.

■ In 1995, 12 people were killed and more than 5,000 injured when **nerve gas** was used in an attack on the Tokyo subway system. The attack was carried out by a religious **cult**.

WHAT ARE TERRORISTS TRYING TO ACHIEVE?

Terrorists have a range of goals. Most organized terrorist groups are driven by a religious or political cause, or a combination of the two. The cause must be powerful enough to prompt people to join a group that is committed to killing civilians to achieve their ends. Groups don't usually force people to become terrorists, so becoming a terrorist is a conscious choice.

In addition to believing in the cause, some people have personality traits that lead them to become terrorists. For example, the appeal of violence might be enough to prompt them to join a terrorist group. In some places, joining a terrorist group may bring status and respect within the community.

Money may also be a reason why some people become terrorists. Many terrorists come from poor communities with high unemployment. Terrorist groups are often well funded, and terrorism may be the only job that seems to be available. Although this may be a factor for some people, it is not a major reason why people turn to terrorism.

CULTS

It is not just the major world religions that attract people who see their teachings as justifying terrorism. There are also smaller cults, which may follow some aspects of major religions. Many of these cults believe that the end of the world is close, and they use this to justify attacks on nonbelievers. Examples include the attack on the Tokyo subway system by the Aum Shinrikyo cult in 1995.

Religious terrorism

We saw in an earlier chapter how the Iranian Revolution and the Soviet invasion of Afghanistan had a big impact on the development of radical Islamist groups. Before those events, most of the world's major terrorist acts had a political motive. Now the motive is more likely to be religious.

Religious terrorism is much more difficult to resolve than terrorism caused by political concerns. The ultimate aim of al-Qaeda is the rule of a single *caliph* or ruler of the Muslim world. People who are prepared to kill others in the name of religion are looking to establish a new society or destroy those who disagree with them. People who believe they are in a struggle of good against evil are much less likely to compromise than a group that has a clear political goal.

Many of the examples in this book concern Islamist terrorism, and most of the recent religious terrorism has been in the name of radical Islam. However, there have been terrorist attacks in the name of most religions at one time or another.

■ Many believe that Islamic schools, called *madrassas*, encourage students to join radical Islamist groups. Others say that most *madrassas* provide good religious schooling for those who might get little or no education.

Those who carry out attacks in the name of religion are usually basing their goals on a selective reading of the sacred texts of that religion. In all major world religions, the vast majority of people are firmly opposed to terrorism.

Political aims

Other causes of terrorism are mainly local. While religious terrorists like al-Qaeda may see their actions as a global struggle, political concerns are often much more local.

Nationalism is a major motive for terrorism. This is the belief that people with a common culture should be able to rule themselves. Nationalism is common in large states that are made up of many different ethnic groups. It is often combined with religion. Different national groups are often united by their religion. Muslim Chechen separatists have fought a long war and terrorist campaign to gain **independence** from largely Christian Russia.

■ Palestinian militants, including suicide bombers, have wide support among their people. They feel they have no other way to fight back against what they see as an illegal occupation by Israel. Israel argues that it cannot discuss a solution while Palestinians are still carrying out terrorist attacks.

TAMIL TIGERS IN SRI LANKA

Another group that combined religious and nationalist grievances were the Hindu Tamils of Sri Lanka. The LTTE, or Tamil Tigers, fought the Buddhist Sinhalese majority for more than 25 years in an effort to set up their own country in the north of Sri Lanka. Their tactics included using suicide bombers as well as their own army and air force. They were finally crushed by the government in 2009.

Drawing national boundaries

Nationalist movements often come about because of history. Before World War I, many countries were part of the empires of European countries. At the end of the war, new national borders were drawn that created large **ethnic minorities** in some countries. These minorities were often very different from the **majority** population, and they wanted their own identity. Governments are usually not happy to let regions have their independence. However, limited **concessions**—such as allowing people to speak their own language or have their own government—will often reduce popular support for extreme nationalists.

Groups wanting independence or their own homeland often do not have the resources to wage a war. They also may not have the support of the majority of the people they claim to represent. This support will often depend on the response of the government they are fighting against. ETA, (see box) which campaigned for a separate state for the Basque people in northern Spain, found that support for their bombing campaign declined when the Spanish government gave the Basque people some freedom to govern themselves.

NATIONALISM IN SPAIN

The group ETA began its campaign for independence for the Basque people, who live in northern Spain and southern France, in the 1960s. Since then, more than 800 people have been killed in ETA attacks. Popular support for the group was once strong but has declined in the twenty-first century. As support declined, there were mass demonstrations against their terrorist attacks. ETA declared a ceasefire in September 2010. Time will tell whether their terror campaign is finally over.

Other political causes have been used to justify terrorism. During the **Cold War**, there were numerous extreme left-wing or **communist** terrorist groups across Europe. Groups like the Red Brigades in Italy believed that their society should be run differently. They thought that terrorist attacks would damage confidence in the government and attract like-minded people to their cause. These groups faded in Europe during the 1980s as the Cold War came to an end and their beliefs seemed outdated. There are still some isolated communist groups, such as the Shining Path terrorist group in Peru and the FARC in Colombia.

"PRO-LIFE" TERRORISTS

Between 1993 and 1994, five hospital workers were shot dead in the United States. Their "crime" in the eyes of those who shot them was that they performed abortions. "Pro-life" terrorists have also been responsible for bomb attacks and for setting fire to abortion clinics. Their Christian beliefs lead them to view abortion as murder of an unborn child. This view is shared by many people, including the **Catholic** Church, but only a small minority resort to terrorism.

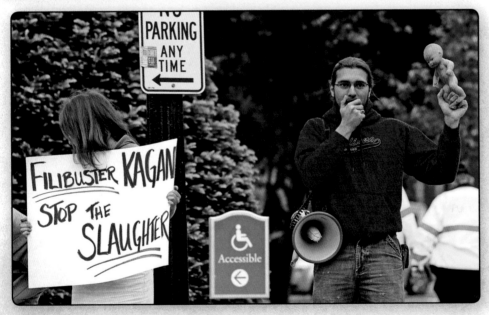

■ Most people express their views peacefully, but there are extremists in some causes who will commit acts of terrorism.

Extreme right-wing groups have also carried out terrorist acts. These include **white supremacist** groups in the United States and **neo-Nazi** groups in Europe. These groups often claim to be following Christian beliefs. They believe that their countries should be racially pure, and they focus their attacks on **immigrants** or ethnic groups within the country. Right-wing or extreme religious groups may also target something they believe to be against Christian teaching, such as homosexuality and **abortion**.

Emotive issues

Terrorist attacks can be motivated by single issues. In both the United States and the United Kingdom, for example, scientific researchers and universities have been targeted by **extremist** animal rights activists. Although attacks are rare and these groups are small, they use terror to discourage scientists from using animals in medical research. Other research institutions have to put in place costly security, which may dissuade them from even supporting the research. Environmentalists have targeted companies that pollute the environment, but, as yet, this has not led to terrorist attacks against people. Extremist groups could be formed on any issue that arouses strong emotions.

Although a tiny minority of people resort to violence, most protest peacefully about their causes. One of the main claims of people who oppose strict laws against terrorists is that those laws may be used to stop people expressing their views peacefully. In a democracy, we have the right to protest about things we disagree with but not to threaten or harm others.

WOMEN AND TERRORISM

Most terrorists are men, but there have been a number of instances of women carrying out terrorist attacks. In the Middle East, women have often carried out suicide bombings. Women are more likely than men to reach their target without being detected. Palestinian Fatma Najar was 70 when she blew herself up in 2006, killing several Israelis. She did this in revenge for the military occupation of the land where she lived and because she had lost family members in the conflict.

CASE STUDY

Swapping the bullet for the ballot box

On the evening of April 10, 1998, a historic agreement was announced. After nearly 30 years of terrorist attacks, leaving more than 3,000 people dead, the conflict in Northern Ireland took a decisive step on the road to peace. In the Good Friday Agreement, the major parties and the British and Irish governments agreed to have an assembly set up to govern Northern Ireland. Terrorist groups on both sides of the conflict committed themselves to giving up violence.

Northern Ireland was created in 1921, when most of Ireland became independent from Great Britain. The majority of the population was **Protestant**. They wanted to remain part of the United Kingdom and Northern Ireland rather than join Ireland, which was mostly Catholic. A minority of the people of Northern Ireland were Catholics, frustrated that they were not part of the new Irish Republic. They felt they were treated as second-class citizens in Protestant-dominated Northern Ireland.

In the late 1960s, violence erupted between the two communities. This led to years of attacks by Republican (Catholic) and Loyalist (Protestant) terrorists. The most prominent group was the Irish Republican Army (IRA), which waged its campaign against the police, army, and civilians in Northern Ireland and Great Britain.

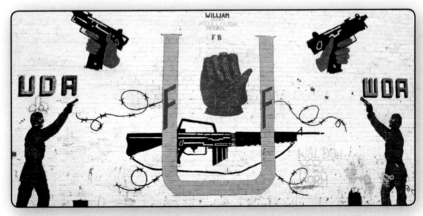

■ Many Loyalist terrorists have also committed themselves to resolving their differences by peaceful means.

Ending the violence

Gerry Adams recognized as early as 1979 that Republicans could not achieve their goals by the use of violence. Adams was the most public face of Sinn Fein, the political wing of the IRA. Many people suspect he held senior positions in the IRA itself. The IRA and Sinn Fein began to develop a political strategy alongside their use of the bullet and the bomb. Sinn Fein and others began to explore possibilities for peace.

The IRA announced a ceasefire in 1994. The ceasefire was broken by a massive bomb in London's Docklands in 1996 that killed two people, but it was restored in 1997. This created the conditions for the talks that led to the Good Friday Agreement. There were many difficulties and disagreements to come, and there were some attacks by small splinter groups of terrorists such as the Real IRA. But the peace has largely held since 1998.

Path to power

Since the Good Friday Agreement, Sinn Fein has become the second largest political party in the Northern Ireland Assembly. Martin McGuinness, who has admitted to being a senior IRA commander in the 1970s, has become deputy first minister of Northern Ireland. The fact that Sinn Fein no longer represents an active terrorist organization has increased its appeal in the Catholic community of Northern Ireland. Many Loyalist terrorists have also committed themselves to resolving their differences by peaceful means.

Gerry Adams (right) and Martin McGuinness were the leaders of Sinn Fein's transition from terrorist mouthpiece to part of the government of Northern Ireland.

REACTING TO TERRORISM

Terrorist attacks are usually designed to get a reaction. For terrorists, the people who are killed and injured in their attacks are often less important than the people who still have to fly on planes knowing that they are targets for terrorists, or the people who watch the attacks unfold on a television screen.

The people who are most immediately affected by terrorism are those caught in the bomb blast or gunfire. The number of people directly affected by a terrorist attack is much wider than we think. The death of anyone in a terrorist attack will have a devastating effect on their family and friends. Those who are injured in terrorist attacks, such as the more than 1,800 people injured in the Madrid bombings (see box), may carry the physical and mental scars for the rest of their lives, including major injuries such as the loss of limbs.

Fear of terrorism

The ripples from a terrorist attack do not stop with those directly involved. One of terrorists' main weapons is the fear they create. In most countries, terrorism is one of the rarest forms of crime. Before the attacks of 9/11, it was not a big concern for most people. Since then, it has been a major concern in most Western countries. We will look later at how governments protect us from terrorism. But regular government warnings about the dangers of terror plots have kept the issue fresh in people's minds.

Fear is just one of the effects of terrorism. Many people's first reaction to a terrorist attack is anger at those who would attack innocent civilians. This anger is another weapon that the terrorists can use. It may become anger against our own government for not stopping the terrorists, as happened in Spain. It may also create tension within the wider population. For example, an Islamist terror attack may lead to a backlash against Muslims, most of whom oppose the attack. Attacks or prejudice against ordinary Muslims will cause them to defend themselves and possibly join the terrorists.

MADRID TRAIN BOMBINGS

One of Europe's worst terrorist disasters happened on March 11, 2004. Several bombs hidden in backpacks were exploded on trains as they arrived in Madrid, Spain, during rush hour.

Some 191 people were killed and more than 1,800 were injured when the bombers struck. Initially, the Spanish government tried to blame the Basque terrorist group ETA for the attacks. It soon became clear that the attackers had been Moroccan Islamist terrorists. In elections just 11 days after the bombings, the government was defeated. People felt that Spain's involvement in the war in Iraq had made the country a target, although investigators found that the bombings had been planned before the start of the war.

"My personality changed. I had a quick temper. I couldn't concentrate. I couldn't even read a newspaper."

Eloy Moran, injured in the Madrid train bombings of March 11, 2004

How the media reacts

Terrorists are very sensitive to mass media, particularly television and, more recently, the Internet. It is no accident that the growth of terrorism from the 1960s on coincided with the appearance of a television in the corner of every family's living room.

While terrorists are skilled in using the media to get their message across, TV channels and newspapers are often happy to cover terrorism. Most newspapers and television channels are driven by the need to reach a lot of people and attract advertisers. There are a number of twenty-four-hour news stations around the world, including CNN, Sky News, and Al Jazeera, which is based in the Middle East. This gives terrorists an outlet for publicizing their actions around the clock.

Terrorists often create their own materials for the media. These include video messages recorded by people like Osama Bin Laden that are circulated on the Internet. Edited versions are often broadcast on TV, and there is some concern that they may contain hidden messages for terrorist cells. Suicide bombers, such as the men who attacked the London transportation system in 2005, may also create video messages before their deaths that are later broadcast by the media.

Bias and censorship

When dealing with emotional issues like terrorism, news organizations are often accused of favoring one side or showing **bias**. At the most basic level, this bias could be in the words that are chosen. Even using the word *terrorist* can be controversial. Western news organizations have often been accused of bias in their coverage of Islamist terrorism. They have also been accused of favoring Israel over the Palestinians. Critics argue that Israel is not as heavily criticized as Palestinian extremists for what they see as terrorism.

Al Jazeera, which broadcasts in Arabic and English, has been accused of anti-Western bias. The station says they are reporting stories or points of view that might be ignored on Western media. Al Jazeera has also been accused of attacking many regimes in the Arab world. One presenter for the station commented, "If we have been accused of being agents of so many regimes, we must be getting it right."

■ The attacks on the World Trade Center on 9/11 were captured live on television, bringing the horrors of international terrorism into millions of homes. The names Osama Bin Laden and al-Qaeda became instantly familiar to people around the world.

DO THE MEDIA HELP TERRORISTS?

There is no doubt that the mass media provide a vital tool for terrorists. Without the media, it would be much more difficult for terrorists to get their message across. The media can also stoke fear of terrorism by speculating about possible attacks in the future. People like Osama Bin Laden have done their best to encourage this speculation.

However, if the media chose not to report terrorist attacks, we would rightly accuse them of bias and not giving us the full story. People may be appalled and turn against the terrorists' cause if they see attacks on TV.

PROTECTING PEOPLE

Up to now, we have looked at the methods that terrorists use and how the general public reacts to them. This chapter will look at how governments protect people from terrorism. What are the options open to them, and how successful are they? Should we be worried that laws to combat terrorism might restrict the rights of all of us in our daily lives?

The rule of law

Democratic governments are normally bound by the **rule of law** when dealing with terrorists. This means that governments have to follow the laws of a country just like everyone else. It is not possible for the U.S. or U.K. governments to go around shooting suspected terrorists or blowing up their hideouts without accounting for their actions. Suspected terrorists have to be arrested and tried by the courts. The fact that governments have to observe the rule of law is important for all of us. If we were arrested for a serious crime, we too would have the opportunity to go to court to protest our innocence.

Many governments choose to treat terrorists as criminals according to the laws of the country. However, terrorists may be in large, well-organized groups that are supported and helped by that country's community. Witnesses will be reluctant to come forward because they fear revenge from other members of the terrorist group. Finally, it may be very difficult to catch the culprits in large-scale attacks like a bomb blast carried out by remote control.

Making concessions

All governments say that they don't negotiate with terrorists, but this often happens anyway, as in Northern Ireland (see pages 26 to 27). Governments do make concessions that will erode the support for terrorism. For example, an ethnic group that wants independence will be less inclined to back terrorists if they are given their own parliament.

Governments and the public need to be constantly on their guard for terrorist attacks. In 2010, a car bomb in New York City's Times Square was spotted by a member of the public. Fortunately, the bomb was poorly made and was made safe before it could explode.

DEBATE

IS IT RIGHT TO NEGOTIATE WITH TERRORISTS?

Arguments for:

- There are many examples of terrorist campaigns that have been ended by negotiation, such as the IRA's campaign in Northern Ireland.

- If negotiating will save lives, then it's the right thing to do. Negotiations may prevent attacks for a time, even if they are not successful.

- Most terrorist groups include some people who are less extreme than others. Negotiating may undermine the power of the extremists.

- Being willing to negotiate just means we are prepared to talk to terrorists. It does not mean giving in to their demands.

Arguments against:

- If terrorists are seen as winning, it will encourage other groups to take up violence.

- Negotiating is a waste of time as terrorists will not compromise.

- If we negotiate, we will be betraying the people who have been killed by the terrorists.

- Terrorists break the law like other criminals, and we do not negotiate with criminals.

CASE STUDY

The war on terror

Another way for governments to deal with terrorists is to declare war on them. This was the option taken by the United States and its allies after the 9/11 attacks.

Anti-terrorist laws

Although democratic governments have to work within the law, they do have the option to change the law to tackle terrorism if existing laws are not sufficient to deal with the threat.

Following the attacks of 9/11, the United States created the Department of Homeland Security. This new body was designed to coordinate the fight against terrorism on U.S. soil. Just six weeks after the attacks, the new U.S.A. PATRIOT Act became law. This was designed to give police and other security forces the powers they felt they needed to combat terrorism. Some of the most controversial parts of the act were that it allowed a big increase in **surveillance** of citizens by police and other agencies. They had greater powers to listen to phone calls and other electronic communication by terrorist suspects. Authorities could also get records from libraries and bookstores showing what suspects were reading.

Other laws that governments have introduced in response to global terrorism include:

- Changing the definition of terrorism so more crimes are covered by anti-terrorist laws
- Imposing stricter controls on foreigners entering the country. This is particularly important if they are believed to hold extreme views that may lead them to support terrorism.
- Banning some things that would not be crimes in other areas—for example, limiting freedom of speech to prevent people "glorifying" terrorism

Civil liberties

Opinions about new anti-terrorist laws are often divided. Groups that campaign for **civil liberties** say that these laws are against our **human rights**, such as:

- If people are arrested, they should be charged or released.
- Everyone has a right to freedom of speech even if we are offended by what someone is saying.
- Anti-terrorism powers are misused to tackle other crimes. For example, people may be searched under anti-terror laws when the police actually suspect them of another crime.

Two views on terrorism

Following the attacks of 9/11, President George W. Bush felt that the best way to deal with terrorism was to go to war against terrorists. Barack Obama, who became president in 2009, has said that he does not believe this is the best way to prevent terrorism.

"Our war on terror begins with al-Qaeda, but it does not end there. It will not end until every terrorist group of global reach has been found, stopped, and defeated."

President George W. Bush, September 2001

"Our long-term security will not come from our ability to instill fear in other peoples but through our capacity to speak to their hopes."

President Barack Obama, May 2010

■ Tony Blair, British prime minister from 1997 to 2007, supported President Bush in declaring war on terror and introducing many new laws to combat it.

People also argue that the laws are out of proportion to the threats we face and that governments exaggerate this threat to restrict our freedoms. The government says that the laws are necessary to protect people. Many people agree, arguing that a small loss of civil liberties is a price worth paying to be safe from terror.

Terrorism threat levels

Many countries, including the United States and the United Kingdom, have introduced a system of warnings about terrorism. These are designed to keep people informed about terrorist activity. The threat level is normally raised after any attack or when security services uncover a terrorist plot. These warning systems are controversial. Since the system was introduced in the United States in 2002, the threat level has never been lower than "Elevated." Levels of "Low" or "Guarded" have never been used. Some people have suggested that the threat levels have been used for political reasons, such as raising the level just before an election in order to stop people from voting for candidates who are not seen as taking a hard line on terrorism.

■ Since 2001, heavily armed police have become a familiar sight at places seen as being at high risk for attack, such as airports.

Police and security

The increased threat of terrorism since 2001 has had an impact on our daily lives in many ways. One response of the government is to make targets hard for terrorists to get to. Airports and airplanes have been targeted in terrorist plots, so security measures have had to be adapted to keep up with the terrorists. In 2006, a plot was discovered to blow up planes using liquids that could be disguised as drinks and then made to explode once on the plane. Security measures were toughened, and passengers were banned from taking most liquids onto planes.

Airports had to adapt again after a bomber attempted to blow up a plane using explosives strapped to his body (see page 4). This led to the introduction of full-body scanners. Developments like this have raised more questions about privacy, although most plane passengers are happy with any development that will make their journey safer.

FEWER CIVIL LIBERTIES: A PRICE WORTH PAYING TO DEFEAT TERRORISTS?

Arguments for:
- Terrorism is such a big threat that we have to give up some of our freedoms to deal with it.
- If we are not terrorists, we have nothing to fear from greater surveillance and measures designed to combat terrorism.
- Having a bit less freedom is a small price to pay for being safer. We are happy to be searched when we board a plane because we know this is to keep us safe.

Arguments against:
- Terrorists want to limit our freedom. If we give up civil liberties, the terrorists are winning.
- Civil liberties have been fought for over the years. They are there to protect us and should not be given away.
- Governments are just using terrorism as an excuse to have greater powers. The threat of terrorism is used to justify laws that are out of proportion to the threat that terrorists pose.

Not everyone is happy with increased security. Opponents argue that measures like full-body scanners make us feel safer but do not really tackle terrorism. Opponents also argue that airports are huge places employing thousands of people, and it is difficult to make them totally secure. Terrorists will find new weaknesses in security.

Security versus lifestyle

Terrorists have shown that they are willing to attack any place where large numbers of people can be found. Plots to attack shopping malls and transportation systems have been uncovered. Well-known buildings and landmarks are also thought to be high on the list of targets. Even if airport security can stop attacks on planes, can we really protect other public places from attack?

There are more surveillance cameras on our streets than ever before. Do they keep us safe or do they just spy on us?

Going through security at an airport is one thing, but would you be happy if you had to go through airport-style security every time you boarded a train or bus, or every time you went into a shopping mall? Are you happy that whenever you are on the street, particularly in busy places, you may be watched by security cameras? These questions and others are likely to come up more often as governments balance the need to protect us from terrorism with the privacy and freedoms we expect as citizens.

Catching suicide bombers

Suicide bombers have been responsible for numerous terrorist attacks in the Middle East. Up to now, there have been few suicide attacks in the West. Attacks like this present huge problems for police, as the tragic example in the box below shows. If police suspect that someone is a suicide bomber, they have to assume that it will not be possible to arrest the bomber without the bomb being detonated.

Should police shoot to kill in cases where suicide bombing is suspected? If the suspect is a suicide bomber, then shooting them may save lives. But there is always the possibility that they are shooting an innocent person. Is it right to abandon the rule of law to possibly save lives?

JEAN-CHARLES DE MENEZES: MISTAKEN IDENTITY

On July 22, 2005, fear of terrorism was at its height in the United Kingdom. The day before, four attempted suicide bomb attacks on the London transportation system had only been prevented because the attackers' bombs failed to explode. Two weeks earlier, 52 people had died in suicide attacks on three underground trains and a bus. Police were hunting the failed suicide bombers. In a tragic case of mistaken identity, Brazilian electrician Jean-Charles de Menezes was shot dead as he sat on an underground train at Stockwell station. Armed police, working under extreme pressure and fearing another attack, wrongly identified Menezes as a suicide bomber. Menezes was a victim of the confusion and fear created by terrorism.

FIGHTING TERRORISM

One of the keys to fighting terrorism is gathering **intelligence**. The U.S. Department of Homeland Security was formed partly to coordinate the gathering and use of intelligence. Security services monitor phone and e-mail communications of thousands of potential suspects to try and pick up any hint of an attack being planned. It has often been said that terrorists only have to get lucky once, whereas security forces have to get it right all the time to prevent terrorist attacks.

Internet communication allows attacks to be planned by terrorists working in different cities or countries. **Encrypted** messages between terrorists are often described as "chatter." These are messages that are sent in code. Although security forces may not be able to decode these messages, they monitor the number of messages sent between known terrorists, as this may tell them if an attack is imminent.

CUTTING TERRORISTS' MONEY SUPPLY

International terrorism costs money. It has been estimated that the operation to hijack planes on 9/11 cost about $500,000, although this was a small amount compared to the damage caused. Some terrorist groups rob banks or commit other crimes to fund their activities. Others, including al-Qaeda and the Palestinian group Hamas, are largely funded by donations. Where bank accounts can be linked to terrorist organizations, governments have tried to get them frozen, to deny these groups the money they need to continue their campaigns.

Issues around intelligence gathering

New laws giving security services more **surveillance** powers have led to fears that these powers are being used for more than just catching terrorists. Some intelligence that has been gathered has also turned out to be incorrect.

Many countries have strict rules on how intelligence can be obtained and what can be used in court. Lots of information comes from intercepting phone calls and e-mails. In some places this is allowed as **evidence** in court. In others, including the United Kingdom, it cannot be used as evidence. This is partly because security services do not want this information to be public—it might give away too much about how they operate. Privacy campaigners argue that too much information is gathered without people's knowledge.

Rules on evidence are also designed to stop information being gained by torture. There have been allegations that some countries have used torture to get information from suspected terrorists, or that suspects have been deliberately moved to countries where torture is allowed, in order to gather information. One such torture technique is waterboarding. Waterboarding involves water being poured repeatedly over the head and face of the suspects so they feel as if they are drowning. In his 2010 book, *Decision Points*, President George W. Bush confirmed and defended his decision to use waterboarding to gain information from an al-Qaeda leader. In 2010, British prime minister David Cameron announced an investigation into whether the United Kingdom may have used evidence obtained by torture.

In 2006, surveillance of e-mails and phone calls enabled security forces to stop a plot to blow up several planes as they flew across the Atlantic Ocean. Several British men linked to al-Qaeda were later convicted of planning the attacks.

Fighting the War on Terror

In September 2001 President George W. Bush declared a war against terrorism, following the attacks by al-Qaeda. The United States was supported by the United Kingdom and many other countries. In October 2001, the first shots were fired in this War on Terror, when al-Qaeda training camps and the bases of the ruling Taliban were attacked in Afghanistan. The main aim of Operation Enduring Freedom was to prevent al-Qaeda from using Afghanistan as a base. The Taliban would also be removed from power.

Ten years later, al-Qaeda has been greatly weakened. Many of its leaders, including Bin Laden, have now been captured or killed. However, it is expected that others will continue to communicate with followers around the world. The Taliban was no longer in power but continued to fight a guerrilla war against allied forces. More than 2,000 allied soldiers had been killed in Afghanistan, and the number of deaths rose every year between 2006 and 2010.

■ Saddam Hussein was tried by his own people in 2006. He was convicted of crimes against humanity and executed on December 30, 2006.

War in Iraq

The War on Terror was extended to Iraq in 2003. The dictator Saddam Hussein was removed from power. As in Afghanistan, initial military success was followed by a long period of guerrilla warfare that claimed thousands of lives, most of them citizens of Iraq. One of the main goals of this war was to find and destroy chemical and biological weapons so they could not be used by Saddam Hussein or any other group. No large quantities of these weapons were found, however, and it seems they were destroyed by the Iraqi leader before the war. In this case, the intelligence reports were wrong. The last U.S. combat troops left Iraq in September 2010.

■ The War on Terror continues in the harsh mountains of Afghanistan.

DEBATE

ARE WESTERN GOVERNMENTS NOT TOUGH ENOUGH ON TERRORISTS?

Arguments for:

- Terrorists will use whatever methods they can, including killing hundreds of innocent people. We need to be just as ruthless to defeat them.
- The rule of law makes it too difficult for Western courts to stop terrorists. Courts need lots of evidence. If terrorists are caught while they are planning an attack, there is often not enough evidence to **convict** them.
- If we have to lose some of our civil liberties to defeat terrorists, that is a small price to pay to prevent terrorist attacks.

Arguments against:

- If we use the same methods as terrorists, such as running the risk of killing more civilians, we are no better than they are.
- We need to treat terrorists like any other criminal. We have strict rules on evidence to stop people being convicted of crimes they did not commit. Even terrorists are innocent until we prove they are guilty.
- Many terrorists believe that our society is weak because of the freedom we have. If we do not follow the rule of law, we are giving in to terrorists who want to damage our society.

Has the war been a success?

There are different views about whether the wars in Afghanistan and Iraq have been successful. We will probably never know how many terrorist attacks have been prevented by the War on Terror. Attacks have continued, but none on the scale of 9/11.

Many people believe that the wars in Afghanistan and Iraq have persuaded Muslims to join groups like al-Qaeda. Videos recorded by suicide bombers have mentioned the wars and the deaths of Muslims as a cause of their actions. Many of those who fought the allies in Iraq came from outside Iraq. But the war has weakened the base of al-Qaeda and its ability to train terrorists. Countries like Libya have stopped their support for terrorism.

The Taliban in Afghanistan and Saddam Hussein in Iraq have been removed from power. However, any benefit for the people of those countries needs to be balanced against the loss of the thousands of civilians killed in the conflicts. Many people question whether the war was justified and whether it made the world a safer place.

Rules of conflict

When countries fight a war, there are certain rules that they follow. These are set out in several agreements that are together known as the **Geneva Convention**. The Geneva Convention distinguishes between **combatants** and **non-combatants** and says that attacks cannot be deliberately launched against non-combatants. Terrorists often deliberately focus their attacks on non-combatants.

There are also rules about how prisoners captured during wartime (prisoners of war) should be treated. In January 2002, the first prisoners arrived at the U.S. Naval Base in Guantanamo Bay, Cuba, after a twenty-hour flight from Afghanistan. These suspected members of al-Qaeda were described as "unlawful enemy combatants," meaning they did not have the same rights as prisoners of war. After a ruling by the U.S. Supreme Court in 2006, the U.S. Defense Department said that all military prisoners were covered by the Geneva Convention. President Obama ordered the gradual closure of Guantanamo Bay prison in January 2009.

Future of the fight against terrorism

After 10 years of fighting in Afghanistan, and with changes in governments in many countries, including the United States, people who supported the war have become concerned about the number of lives that have been and are still being lost. This conflict may seem far away, but governments would argue that, without the efforts of troops in Afghanistan, we would have seen more attacks like the ones that struck the United States in 2001 and have struck many countries, including the United Kingdom, since that time.

There were allegations that extreme methods, called "torture" by human rights groups, were used to get information from prisoners held at Guantanamo Bay.

"I feel responsibility but no regret for removing Saddam Hussein. I think he was a monster. I believe he threatened not just the region but the world."
Tony Blair, former British prime minister, speaking in January 2010

TACKLING THE CAUSES OF TERRORISM

It is natural for people to dismiss terrorists as "evil" or "monsters" immediately after a terrorist attack. However, when we get over the emotional impact of the attack, it is possible to see that there may be some general reasons why these acts were committed that are separate from religious or political motivation. Many people believe that there would be fewer terrorist attacks if the international community had more success in tackling these general issues, although not all of the issues apply to all terrorist groups.

Unstable countries

Terrorist movements are often able to base themselves in countries that have weak government control because of war or other reasons. Afghanistan has been at war, either with other countries or between internal tribes, almost ever since it was invaded by the Soviet Union in 1979. This has meant that people in Afghanistan have become used to conflict and being isolated from the modern world. This has provided a base for terrorists.

If places like Afghanistan were provided with more foreign aid to provide education, health care, and a stable government, would people be less likely to support terrorists? Western powers would argue that this is already happening. Unfortunately, civilians are still being killed by both sides in the conflict.

Does **poverty** itself cause people to turn to terrorism? There is little evidence that this is a major cause. However, unfair distribution of wealth and power are often factors. If one group or country is seen to be gaining wealth and power at the expense of another, this could lead to terrorism.

Clash of civilizations

Some argue that civilizations are opposed to each other for cultural reasons. This view means that no matter how much wealth and power are distributed around the world, different people will always be at odds. Greater understanding of other cultures might help to deal with this. However, this theory ignores the fact that most terrorist groups are actually fighting for local issues such as nationalism rather than carrying out general attacks on the West like al-Qaeda and its supporters.

■ The United Nations Security Council is the main global body for resolving disputes between nations. Some of the underlying causes of terrorism require global action.

PEACE IN THE MIDDLE EAST

Many people agree that it will be impossible to end global terrorism without some kind of solution to the conflict between Israel and the Palestinians. The lack of progress on this issue is one major reason for opposition to Western countries by Muslims, who believe that the West favors Israel. Many U.S. and European leaders recognize this, and President Barack Obama has publicly supported a Palestinian state.

"It is in the interests not only of the Palestinians but also the Israelis, the United States, and the international community to achieve a two-state solution."

Is the world a safer place?

The battle against global terrorism is far from over. The aim of the security measures and military action against terrorists is to make the world a safer place. Huge resources have been devoted to tackling terrorist suspects and preventing attacks since 2001.

There are some reasons to believe that we are safer from terrorism now than we have been in the past. We are more aware of the dangers, and potential terrorists are being monitored all the time. Security at places like airports is much tighter than it was in the past. War in Afghanistan has disrupted the main base of al-Qaeda and restricted its ability to train terrorists.

IS TERRORISM SOMETIMES JUSTIFIED?

Arguments for:

- Terrorist groups would argue that they are fighting a war and they are justified because they are fighting for a greater good.
- It has often been said that "one person's terrorist is another person's freedom fighter." Many people who have been called terrorists by their opponents have wide support with a particular group of people.
- For some people, terrorism is the only way they can fight back against a cruel government or an invasion by another country.
- Governments will often say that it is justifiable to kill civilians if the end result benefits people. Is this very different from terrorism?

Arguments against:

- Whatever arguments terrorists use to justify themselves, their actions are criminal.
- Although some people may see a terrorist campaign as fighting for freedom, it does not alter the fact that they are targeting civilians.
- There is always a better approach than terrorism. If people resort to terrorism, they are as bad as the cruel government they are opposing.
- Democratic governments are justified if they kill civilians for a greater good because a majority of people voted for them. If governments deliberately target civilians, this is state terrorism and is not justified.

However, those who say we are not safer argue that the conflict since 2001 has not addressed many of the underlying causes of international terrorism. The number of young radical Muslims who are angry about Western influence and are prepared to commit terror attacks may have increased. Governments are still worried about the possibility that terrorists could get access to WMDs. Al-Qaeda still exists and there are also other terrorist campaigns going on in different regions around the world (see pages 50 to 51).

■ Nelson Mandela, the former president of South Africa, is admired around the world for uniting all the people in his country after being jailed for decades by the former government. At the time of his imprisonment in 1962, Mandela had been involved in violence against the government, and many people saw him as a terrorist.

What do you think?

Many of the issues and debates raised by terrorism and how we respond to it are not going to go away. We know that the arguments on both sides will change over time. Terrorist campaigns that seem impossible to solve now will be resolved over time as the people involved change.

Do we think that the measures taken since 2001 will make us safer? Should we negotiate with terrorists or try to defeat them by force? Much of our response depends on whether we believe that the terrorist challenge the world faces in the twenty-first century is different and more dangerous than any previous terrorism.

■ Terror attacks in Mumbai, India, in 2008 were a deadly reminder of the danger of terrorism.

TERRORISM AROUND THE WORLD

This table shows examples of some of the terrorist campaigns around the world. This list does not include all terrorist organizations.

Terrorist campaign	Location	Details	Aims
Al-Qaeda	Global, main base in Afghanistan/ Pakistan	Founded in late 1980s by Osama Bin Laden, linked to many groups across the world. Believed to be responsible for many global terror attacks including attacks on New York and Washington, D.C., on September 11, 2001.	Removal of Western influence from Muslim countries. Establishment of Islamic *caliphate* across the Muslim world
Aum Shinrikyo	Japan	Religious cult responsible for nerve gas attack on Tokyo subway in 1995. Claims to have abandoned violence.	To take over Japan and the world
ETA (Basque Fatherland and Liberty)	Spain	Formed in 1959, ETA's attacks have included bombing and assassination aimed at the Spanish government and bombings of tourist areas.	An independent Basque homeland in what is now northern Spain and south-western France
FARC (Revolutionary Armed Forces of Colombia)	Colombia	Formed in 1964, FARC is responsible for bombings and kidnappings in Colombia. Numbers have been reduced since 2000 by government forces.	Replace the current government with a communist regime
GIA and GSPC	Algeria	Formed in 1992 when an extreme Islamic party was outlawed in Algeria. Responsible for the murder of many Algerian civilians.	Establish an Islamic state in Algeria

Hamas	Occupied Territories (Gaza and the West Bank)	The largest of many Palestinian terrorist groups in the Occupied Territories. Methods include suicide bombings in Israel. Hamas has wide support among Palestinians and was voted the largest party in the Occupied Territories in 2006 elections.	Establish an Islamic Palestinian state in place of Israel
Liberation Tigers of Tamil Eelam (LTTE), also known as the Tamil Tigers	Sri Lanka	Established 1976, the Tamil Tigers has had strong support among Sri Lanka's minority Tamil population. Military defeat by government forces in 2009. It remains to be seen whether their terrorist campaign is over.	Establish an independent Tamil state in the north of Sri Lanka
Moro National Liberation Front and Abu Sayyaf Group	Philippines	Armed conflict has lasted for decades in the southern Philippines, although the government has given some self-government to the region. Abu Sayyaf has links to al-Qaeda.	Establish an Islamic state in Muslim areas of southern Philippines
PKK (Kurdistan People's Party)	Turkey	The PKK began its armed campaign in 1984. It has used the mountains of northern Iraq to launch bombing attacks against Turkey.	More rights and self-government for Kurds living in Turkey (dropped demand for independence in 2004)
Hizbul Mujahideen, Lashkar-e-Taiba, Harkatul Mujahideen, Jaish-e-Mohammad	India/ Pakistan	These groups have been responsible for conflict with Indian troops and attacks on civilians in India, including the attacks on Mumbai in 2008. Support has historically come from Pakistan.	Indian-controlled Kashmir to become part of Pakistan
Real IRA	Northern Ireland (UK)	One of a number of splinter groups formed after the Provisional IRA ceasefire in 1998. Claimed responsibility for a bomb in Omagh, Northern Ireland, in 1998 that killed 29 people.	For Northern Ireland (part of the United Kingdom) to be united with the Republic of Ireland

GLOSSARY

abortion pregnancy that is terminated in its early stages. People who oppose abortion believe this is murder of an unborn child.

ally country connected to another by an agreement or treaty

assassin person who kills someone for political reasons

atrocity terrible or cruel crime

bias prejudice in favor of one side or the other in an argument

Catholic follower of the Roman Catholic Church, which is a branch of Christianity

civilian anyone who is not a member of the armed forces

civil liberties freedoms that we all have guaranteed by the law, including freedom to say and think whatever we want

combatant person or country ready to engage in or engaged in fighting

communist someone who believes that all property should be controlled by the government, with everyone working for the state. There were communist governments in much of eastern Europe, the Soviet Union, and China during the second half of the twentieth century.

concession making a compromise to reach an agreement

convict prove that someone has committed a crime

cult small group that follows specific beliefs or religions

democratic describing a form of government that is voted for by the people of a country or region

encrypt put information into code so it cannot be read by anyone apart from the person or website you are sending it to

ethnic minority group of people who share a background or culture different from the main culture of a country. An ethnic minority might be made up of recent immigrants.

evidence information that proves something, particularly information that can be used in court to prove that someone has committed a crime

extremist anyone who holds extreme religious or political views

Geneva Convention series of agreements between countries that state how prisoners of war and those injured in wartime should be treated

guerrilla any group engaging in irregular fighting, usually against a larger force or invading army

hijack seize control of an aircraft or building

hostage someone who is captured and used as a way of bargaining by his or her captors

human rights rights that every person has, regardless of who they are or where they live

immigrant someone who was born in a different country to the one in which they now live

independent when something or someone stands on its own. When a country becomes independent of another country, it has its own government.

intelligence information, especially if it is for military or political uses

IRA (Irish Republican Army) military part of Sinn Fein, which aimed for union between the Republic of Ireland and Northern Ireland. After many years of terrorist activity in Northern Ireland and Britain it announced in 2005 that it had ended its military campaign.

Islamist following Islam, usually a particularly strict or conservative form of Islam

jihad Arabic word for a holy war

kidnap hold someone prisoner against their will

majority the biggest part of something

martyrdom when a person dies for his or her beliefs and is then celebrated by people who share those beliefs

nationalism strong patriotic feelings for a country. Nationalism may involve wanting independence from another country.

neo-Nazi person who adopts the extreme racist views of the Nazi party that ruled Germany in the 1930s and 1940s

nerve gas chemical weapon that attacks the nervous system and can cause serious injury or death

non-combatant civilian or someone who is not involved in a conflict

occupy invade and rule a country, often against the will of the people of that country

poverty lack of money or possessions

Protestant someone who follows a branch of Christianity other than the Roman Catholic Church

racist someone who discriminates against people because of where they come from or the color of their skin

refugee person who is forced to move from home because of war or out of fear of being harmed

rule of law system of government in which the law is the final authority. Governments and security services need to obey the law like anyone else.

suicide bomber someone who sets off an explosion designed to kill himself as well as his victims

surveillance watching someone closely, particularly if the person is suspected of a crime

United Nations organization that includes most countries in the world and was formed after World War II to manage disputes between countries and prevent wars

Weapons of Mass Destruction (WMDs) chemical, biological, and nuclear weapons that can cause widespread death and destruction

white supremacist racist who believes that white people are superior to all other races

FURTHER INFORMATION

Books

Brezina, Corona. *Public Security in an Age of Terrorism*. New York: Rosen Publishing, 2009.

Freedman, Jeri. *America Debates Civil Liberties and Terrorism*. New York: Rosen Publishing, 2008.

Katz, Sam. *U.S. Counterstrike: American Counterterrorism*. Terrorism Dossiers. Minneapolis: 21st Century Books, 2005.

Langley, Andrew. *Should We Negotiate with Terrorists?* What Do You Think? Chicago: Heinemann Library, 2008.

Price, Sean Stewart. *Osama Bin Laden*. Front-Page Lives. Chicago: Heinemann Library, 2010.

Various authors, Terrorism series, Mankato, MN: Compass Point Books , 2010. Titles in series: *Combating Terrorism, History of Terrorism, Terrorist Groups, What Makes a Terrorist?*

Websites

Most major news organizations will include regular coverage of terrorist attacks and issues. Some of the most reliable are:

topics.nytimes.com/top/reference/timestopics/subjects/t/terrorism/index.html
The *New York Times* section on terrorism

topics.cnn.com/topics/terrorism
Cable News Network (CNN) site containing news and videos on terrorism

International sites with detailed information on terrorism include:

news.bbc.co.uk/1/hi/in_depth/world/2001/war_on_terror/default.stm
British Broadcast Corporation (BBC)'s news site with detailed information and archives about terrorism, includes page on the war on terror and al-Qaeda

english.aljazeera.net
Al Jazeera, the English version of the Arabic language news network, based in the Middle East presents views that are different than many Western news organizations.

www.dhs.gov/index.shtm
The Department of Homeland Security is the U.S. government department responsible for countering terrorism.

There are also many groups campaigning on particular issues related to terrorism, such as the American Civil Liberties Union (www.aclu.org) and Amnesty International (www.amnesty.org).

Remember that news organizations and websites may report a particular view of the issues. You should look at a number of sources to get a balanced picture of any hot topic.

Topics for further research

- Islam and the Islamic world: This book includes many examples of groups who have committed terrorist attacks which they say are in the name of Islam. However, the views of these people do not represent the majority of Muslims. The history and culture of Islam is a fascinating topic for study, as are the history and culture of countries like Afghanistan.

- The Arab-Israeli conflict and tensions in the Middle East have been the root cause of many terrorist campaigns since World War II. Find out more about this conflict, the reasons for it, and why it is so difficult to solve.

INDEX